马丁·路德·金

Heroes and Role Models | Non-Fiction Series

Copyright © 2022 by Level Learning, INC. and Washington Yu Ying PCS™
Original and Edited Text Copyright © 2022 by Washington Yu Ying PCS™

All rights reserved. No part of this book in whole or part may be reproduced without written permission from the publisher.

Published by Level Learning, INC.
Content Contributors:
Washington Yu Ying PCS™ - Teng Shen, Pearl Zao He You
Level Learning - Jingyao Qi

Illustrations by: Matt Austin

Leveling classification based on Level Learning standard. For full description, visit www.levellearning.com

ISBN 978-1-64040-019-1
Simplified Chinese Edition

About Level Learning:

Level Learning provides a literacy focused curriculum specifically designed for K-12 Chinese as a Second Language classrooms. Our program offers 20 levels of specific and detailed objectives, leveled texts and passages, mastery-based online assessment, and analytics to enable data-driven instruction. Level Learning reading curriculum for both literature and informational text emphasize grammar and comprehension skills to help teachers develop confident and independent Chinese language readers. The non-fiction series of books are specifically designed to support our informational text course based on multiple national standards. To learn more about our entire offering, visit www.levellearning.com.

About Washington Yu Ying PCS™:

Washington Yu Ying PCS is a Mandarin English dual language immersion International Baccalaureate (IB) World school. Yu Ying's mission is to inspire and prepare young people to create a better world by challenging them to reach their full potential in a nurturing Chinese/English educational environment. Yu Ying's comprehensive IB, dual immersion curriculum equips students with global competencies for success in the real world. As a leader in immersion education, Yu Ying is determined to advance Chinese language programs and global citizenry education by helping other schools create and strengthen their Chinese programs. For more information, email: products@washingtonyuying.org

马丁·路德·金出生在美国的一个非洲裔家庭。

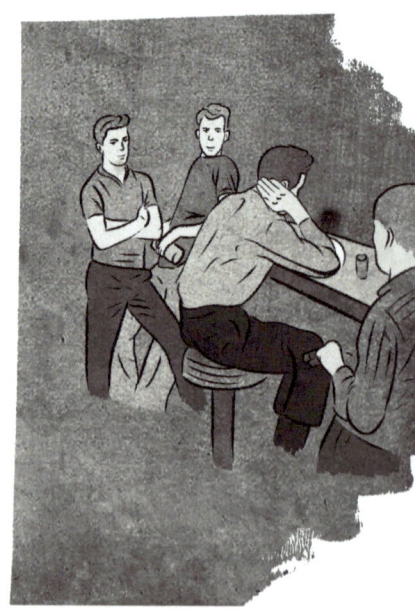

在他小时候，非洲裔不能去白人的商店买东西;非洲裔不能去白人的饭店吃饭;非洲裔也不能去白人的学校学习。

马丁希望有一天,世界上所有的人都是平等的。

长大以后,马丁到处演讲,组织游行。他用非暴力的方式告诉人们,什么是公平和平等。

那时,在公交车上,白人可以坐在前排,非洲裔只能坐后排。一个非洲裔女子因为**拒绝**给白人让座,被警察抓走了。

马丁知道后，马上组织了抗议游行。在之后的一年多里，很多人都拒绝坐公交车。后来，非洲裔在公交车上可以自由地选择座位。

马丁做过很多次演讲，其中最著名的是"我有一个梦想"。1963年8月28日，25万不同肤色、不同种族的人来到华盛顿纪念碑前。马丁告诉全世界他有一个梦想，他希望不同种族的人能平等地生活。

马丁的努力推动了美国的种族平等。1964年，马丁得到了"诺贝尔和平奖"。

为了纪念马丁·路德·金作出的贡献,每年一月的第三个星期一被定为"马丁·路德·金日"。

Glossary

	Pinyin	English Definition
非洲裔	fēi zhōu yì	African descent
平等	píng děng	fair, equal
演讲	yǎn jiǎng	speech
组织	zǔ zhī	to organize
游行	yóu xíng	parade
非暴力	fēi bào lì	non-violent
公平	gōng píng	fairness
拒绝	jù jué	to refuse
抗议	kàng yì	protest
自由	zì yóu	free
种族	zhǒng zú	race
华盛顿	huá shèng dùn	Washington
纪念碑	jì niàn bēi	monument
推动	tuī dòng	to promote
诺贝尔和平奖	nuò bèi ěr hé píng jiǎng	Nobel Peace Prize

	Pinyin	English Definition
纪念	jì niàn	to commemorate
贡献	gòng xiàn	contribution

www.ingramcontent.com/pod-product-compliance
Lightning Source LLC
Chambersburg PA
CBHW041224070526
44584CB00001B/79